NUMMER-HISTORIEN

THE NUMBER STORY

SMALL BOOK ONE

ENGLISH - NORWEGIAN

Numbers Teach Children
Their Number Names

written and illustrated by

MISS ANNA

Early Reader Edition of *The Number Story 1*
Bronze Medal Winner, 2016 Wishing Shelf Book Award

Library of Congress Control Number: 2018902040

Names: Miss Anna, author.
Title: Number story : numbers teach children their number names / Miss Anna.
Description: Portland, OR: Lumpy Publishing, 2018.
Identifiers: ISBN 978-1-945977-36-7 | LCCN 2018902040
Summary: The pictures and rhymes present stories which introduce numbers 0-10.
Subjects: LCSH Numeration—English--Norwegian--Pictorial works--Juvenile literature. | BISAC JUVENILE NONFICTION /
Languages: English--Norwegian
Classification: LCC QA141.3 .M57 2018 | DDC 513—dc23

Publisher: Lumpy Publishing
Website: www.missannabooks.com
Email: missanna@missannabooks.com

Paperback: ISBN 978-1-945977-36-7
Printed in the U.S.A.   1 3 5 7 9 10 8 6 4 2

Har du lyst til å lære navnene til numrene?

It is very easy and a lot of fun!

Det er veldig lett og veldig gøy!

Say-along our little jingle

Syng vår lille historie med oss!

starting from Number One!
Vi vil begynne med Nummer Én.

1
ONE   looks like my one finger.

ÉN

ser ut som min ene finger.

1
ONE!
ÉN!

2
TWO   trails a tail.
TO
lager en hale.

A TAIL! EN HALE!

3

THREE has bumps.

TRE

har humper.

BUMPY! HUMPETE!

4
FOUR carries a sail.
FIRE
bærer et seil.

A SAIL!
ET SEIL!

5
FIVE   is a racing track.
FEM
er en recerbane.

VROOM
BROOMM!

SIX curves like a snail.

SEKS

kurver seg som en snegle.

A SNAIL!   EN SNEGLE!

7

SEVEN has a sharp angle.

SYV

har en skarp vinkel.

BE CAREFUL! IT'S SHARP!
Vær forsiktig! Den er Skarp!

8

EIGHT is rollercoaster rails.

ÅTTE

er rulleskøyteskinner.

JIPPIII!
YIPPEE!

9

NINE is a bubble on a stick.

NI

er en boble på en pinne.

A BUBBLE! EN BOBLE!

10

TEN is an eye of a whale.

TI

er et øye på en hval.

WINK!
BLUNK!
HELLO! HALLO!

And
Og

0

ZERO   is an empty pail.

NULL

er et tomt spann.

IT'S EMPTY!
DET ER TOMT!

Thank you for playing with us today.

We had a lot of fun too!

Takk for at du lekte med oss i dag.

Vi hadde det veldig gøy også!

We are your Number friends,
Zero to Ten,
Who will be here for you~
Vi er Nummervennene dine
Null til Ti.
Vi vil alltid være her for deg.

Bye-bye now!
See you again soon.
Ha det bra så lenge!
Ser deg igjen snart!

The Numbers are *SINGING* too!

To sing-a-long, look for Miss Anna Number Story
at your favorite music store like iTUNES.

MP3

Numbers 0-10
IDENTIFYING
& COUNTING

Numbers 11-20
& Ordinals
first, second, third...

Numbers 0-100
& Place Values
ones, tens, hundreds...

About Clocks
& Telling Time
hours, minutes, seconds...

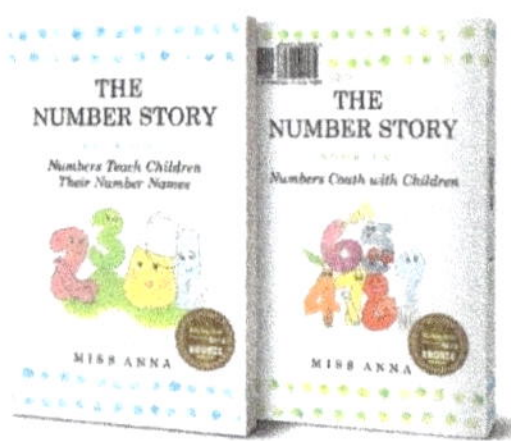

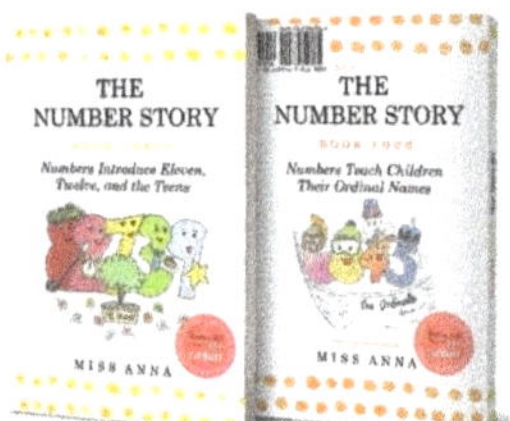

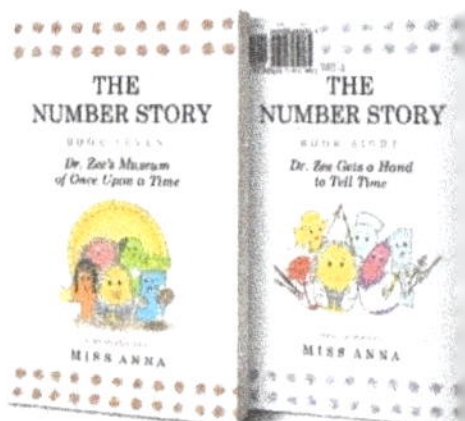

Number Story 1 & 2
isbn: 978-0-996216-48-7

Number Story 3 & 4
isbn: 978-1-945977-01-5

Number Story 5 & 6
isbn: 978-1-945977-06-0

Number Story 7 & 8
isbn: 978-1-949320-40-

For more Miss Anna books to love,
visit us at

www.missannabooks.com

Numbers are working hard all over the world!
Come Travel the World with Us!

9 781945 977367